Third Wednesday
Volume XV
Winter, 2022

Third Wednesday is a quarterly journal of literary and visual arts. Though we manage the magazine from Michigan, we welcome submissions from all over the world. Digital issues of the magazine are completely free to anyone and print issues can be purchased at Amazon.com.

Find us on the web at **thirdwednesdaymagazine.org**. There you can download free digital issues, read the fine poems we have published in the past and find the link to our portal at *Submittable* where you can submit your work and subscribe to the magazine. You can also find and follow us on Facebook, YouTube, Instagram and Tumblr.

Masthead

David Jibson, Editor
Laurence W. Thomas, Editor Emeritus
Judith Jacobs, Art Editor
John F. Buckley, Fiction Editor
Marilyn L. Taylor, Associate
Lynn Gilbert, Associate
Carl Fanning, Associate
Phillip Sterling, Associate
Joe Ferrari, Consulting Editor

Cover Art:
No Strings Attached
Digital Collage
David Jibson / Ann Arbor, Michigan

Table of Contents

Editor's Note for Winter, 2022...4
Pearls / Corey Mesler..5
Sculling on Tawas Bay / Richard Douglass..6
Grand Haven Train / Kimberly Shyu...7
Advice / Terry Belew...8
Banana Wars / Gary Wadley...10
Gibson House Window / Ann Privateer...13
Peaches / January Pearson...14
Edgar, Later (D.W. Griffith, 1909) / Nina Rao..................................15
Autumn, Fall / Robert Nisbet...16
Just Off the High Street / Robert Nisbet...17
Branches and Windows / Christopher Woods..................................18
In Margherita's Kingdom / Cate McGowan.....................................19
That December / Peggy Hammond..20
L'Amour / Jane Blanchard...21
Must Be the Wind / Jack Granath...22
Painting Woman / Rana Williams...23
Time at the River / Mary McCarthy..24
Dandelion / Leslie Schultz...25
Formal Imitation / Mark Mitchell...26
I Spent the Day in Armageddon / Emily Eddins..............................27
To the Cats That Slink Out of Sight When I'm Walking in the Early Morning / Tom Large...28
Lord, Just Give Me One More Spring / Grey Held...........................29
It Was the Cauliflower That Kept Me From Sleep / Babo Kamel..30
When I Stop Being Her Daughter / Babo Kamel.............................31
City Snow / Margaret Birth..32
Sweeping Under the Rug / Gary Bloom...33
Facsimile / Ruth Bavetta..34
Light Likes / Ryan Brennan..34
Plumbing / Sally Zakariya...35
Walk, Swim, Fly / Sally Zakariya..36
Salad Nicoise, 2019 / Sinclair Buckstaff..37
The Seventh Age / Hattie Clarke..40
Autumn, Departures / Robert Haight...41
An Empty Field / Robert Haight...42

Angel of Death / Mary Stebbins Taitt..43
Old Man Taking Account / Darrell Petska..44
Everything Depends on the Day You Ask Me / Ronda Broatch......45
Growing Gone / Kevin Brown..46
Deer in the Yard / J. R. Solonche..48
I Do Not Wish Them Ill / J. R. Solonche...49
Interiors / David Chorlton..50
Monarch / David Chorlton..51
Away We Go / Robert Bulman..52
Micro-sociology / R. A. Allen..53
Landing in Is / Lily Jarman-Reisch..54
Christmas Crow / Lynn White..55
Think (Always) / Patricia Bingham..56
Moth Wings / Laura Ann Reed...57
Splintered White Picket Fence / Victoria Melekian.........................58
Love Blind / Shannon Hollinger...59
Do the Storms Still Reach You? / John Tustin..................................61
Words / Gary Wadley..62
Dad and the Gates of Hell / Ruth Holzer..63
The Greyhound / Graham C. Goff..64
Night Blizzard / Richard Schiffman..66
First Love / Richard Schiffman..67
Boot Jack / Donald Wheelock..68
Being Born / Jeremiah Durick..69
Clue of Home / J. S. Absher...70
I Knew Bobolinko in High School / Kenneth Pobo..........................72
Women These Days / Sarah Iler..73
The Snake Man's Lesson / Robert Fillman.......................................74
Team Captain / Virginia Smith...75
Drawing 2 / John Loree..76

Editor's Note for Winter, 2022

This issue marks a substantial change in the way we publish 3rd Wednesday. We look for ways to expose our contributors to an ever wider audience, and beginning with this issue, the first of our 15th year, each of the poetry pieces included was posted on our website with a brief biography of the contributor as the piece was selected.

Our website is a busy place with lots of followers and traffic. Now, when someone lands on our page, the most recently selected pieces appear in a clickable list at the top of the page's right hand column. In this way individual poems are getting hundreds of views and the change seems to have spurred hundreds more downloads of free digital issues of the magazine.

This change makes it possible for contributors to share their work with family and friends through links on their own social media. We actively encourage this. Spread the word, share the good news and your fantastic work.

The question arises, will publishing everything online before the print issue comes out mean people won't buy or subscribe to the magazine? The answer is we don't know or care. We don't care about selling magazines or subscriptions as much as we care about our contributors being read as widely as possible.

Okay, we have the worst business model imaginable and we'll continue to be bad at business for the foreseeable future.

Enjoy this issue. We've put some nice things in it for you, including the winner of this issue's 50/50 contest, Leslie Schultz of Northfield, Minnesota. Leslie served as guest associate editor for the Winter 2021 issue.

Next up, the spring issue will feature our annual poetry contest which will be taking entries until February 15th. We're really excited to have Keith Taylor serving as judge this time. Support us with an entry.

Pearls / Corey Mesler

My mother did not save much except
money. She was not nostalgic.
There are no drawings I did in
fifth grade, no old report cards, no
favorite toys. I miss my Matchbox
and Corgi cars, my Beatles 45s
on Capitol, my old Mad Magazines
and Ripley's Believe it or Not
paperbacks. All gone to garbage
trucks or garage sales. She handed
little down. I have a couple of my
father's WWII medals, but none
of his letters home. My mother gave
my wife her string of pearls. It is
this one gift I want to talk about.
Tight with money her entire life she
was overly generous at the end. My
wife and I don't go out much. We
don't entertain. But there was an event
where we dressed up, a speech I
had to make. I found my old suit,
purchased at the Salvation Army to
get married in. My wife wore a simple
black dress and upon the breast she
laid that single strand of pearls.
They were like small lights, like prayer
beads, like dreamstuff. They were like
my mother, simple, surviving, hanging on.

   Corey Mesler / Memphis, Tennessee

Sculling on Tawas Bay / Richard Douglass
August 2021

Glistening calm as the sun breaks over the far horizon
Not a ripple, not a wave, not a crest or movement
Faint late summer fog rising
As if the mass of water was silenced for a moment in time

Stroking easily, 18 feet of ash wings
Catch, draw, pull, catch, repeat - rhythm of movement
The sliding seat in opposition to the draw on oars
The touch of blade to water

Behind me a sweeping arch
My wake, nearly delicate, marked on each side
Parallel pools of disturbed water
Blade markers of my path, a pattern of my past

The horizon now glowing with sunlight
The stillness on the shore
Now strays into morning,
the moment has passed into a day

    Richard Douglass / Tawas City, Michigan

Grand Haven Train / Kimberly Shyu

Photograph

Kimberly Shyu / Chantilly, Virginia

Advice / Terry Belew

You should avoid staring at the sun
           during an eclipse unless impulse consumes you.
     You should only think of childhood
            after eating hallucinogens.

You should anticipate
        chemical reactions.
     You should never tell the patrolman
            there's a gun in your trunk.

You should act thankful
         for your speeding ticket.
     You should drive off slowly,
            then speed again because you're late.

You should change your oil, 10w30
          for winter and summer and anytime
     You should somehow translate
           this to blessings, amen.

You should remember that your parents tried
          going to a Methodist church before
    they divorced, how the elderly
           reached out their hands.

You should avoid blessings
         because they are usually selfish.
     You should avoid stubbing
            your toe on religious texts.

You should avoid stubbing
                your toe on living room walls.
      You should remember
                the time the grill caught fire

and dad put water on it and the fire got worse
                so the vinyl siding melted.
      You should be grateful for your cheeseburger.
      You should always be happy

for your cheeseburgers. You should always
                look in the rearview mirror
      to make sure you are not leaking anything.
            You should get the tires rotated.

You should drive away
                but mind what follows you.

    Terry Belew / Bland, Missouri

Banana Wars / Gary Wadley

There is a long history of Gog and Magog: some say they were individuals, some say peoples, some say lands, but this is the truth and Magog would tell you the truth hurts.

Gog lived in a valley and Magog lived on a nearby mountain. They weren't much to look at – hairy and stinking with bad teeth, but they lived mostly outside and had to hustle to stay alive. Their mates looked about the same, only they had boobies.

Gog and Magog got along fairly well, and only occasionally came to blows. Gog was jealous of the mountain, because it was cool in the summer, and Magog was jealous of the valley because it had a nice river with sweet water for drinking and bathing. Each wanted what the other had. They were, after all, men.

Every now and then Gog would climb the mountain or Magog would descend into the valley and the two would drink the fermented juice of berries. At first meeting, they were happy to see each other and discussed mundane things like how many toes does a sloth have or do birds go underground in the winter. They both felt that the fermented juice increased their intelligence, though they could not have explained this.

As they continued to drink the fermented juice, they would grow angry and begin to fight. They would slap each other on the head (they hadn't invented fists yet), but generally did very little damage. Then they would both go home where their hairy wives would scold them by making clucking sounds, then pack mud on their cuts and bruises. They were both dense and their wives would have divorced them, but divorce hadn't been invented yet either.

Fruit grew well in Gog's valley, and one day he got an idea as he was eating a banana: he would bring bananas to his next meeting with Magog, and instead of slapping him on the head he would throw bananas at him from a safe distance. Magog didn't mind this (unless the fruit hit him in the eye), because bananas didn't grow at high altitudes and he would just eat them later. Though unintentional, Gog was sharing his food.

Then one day banana season was over and Gog decided he could also throw squash and mangoes and avocados. True, Magog could eat these also, but if you ever get hit with a well-thrown mango... well...it hurts!

After a particularly heavy bout of increasing their intelligence with fermented juice, Gog threw a hard winter squash at Magog and hit him in the testicles. This is always funny on You Tube, but it's really not. No one would laugh at a woman getting smashed in the boobies. Like divorce, You Tube hadn't been invented yet. Still, Gog fell on the ground laughing. Magog fell on the ground rolling in pain.

"Awwwwwww," yelled Magog (vocabulary was somewhat limited then). The sound echoed over the mountain and down into the valley so that the women lifted their hairy heads and were frightened. Even Gog grew frightened. It was like the sound of birth.

Finally, Magog sat up, grabbed the first thing he saw (a rock) and flung it at Gog. It hit him in the head. "Awwwwww," said Gog, then his eyes crossed and he fell face down in the dirt. Magog waited, but Gog did not move again.

Something had changed. Magog grabbed his mate and kids and moved to a far-off mountain to hide. He didn't know why, he just thought it a good idea. But it didn't do any good.
Gog's mate and kids found his body and the killing rock and figured out what had happened. It was if something else had been launched along with the flying fruit and the rock. Maybe this is what Magog had sensed. It was in the air.

"A little yeast leaveneth the whole lump," Magog used to say as an old and unhappy man when he drank too much fermented juice. No one knew what that meant.
Well...you know the rest: arrows and spears, slings and cannonballs, television and politicians, gain-of-function research and lawyers...La-De-Da.

The Magogites still live in the mountains and the Gogites still live in the valleys. They still drink fermented berry juice, think themselves intelligent, and throw things.

Research indicates the root word *Gog* translates to your last name.

Or maybe not.

True story.

   Gary Wadley / Louisville, Kentucky

Gary's story was an Honorable Mention from our recent George Dila Memorial Flash Fiction Contest.

Gibson House Window / Ann Privateer

Photograph

Ann Privateer / Davis, California

Peaches / January Pearson

When a peach falls
from a tree, wrapped
in its velvet shawl,
plumped with juice,
it reaches its pinnacle.
How different for us.
Slouching on the floral couch,
my grandmother, 102, fiddle
with her blouse, wonders
if someone will sew
a button where she found
three limp strings.
Through the screen door,
she watches woodpeckers
she can't hear, her ear
a broken bell. She gums
a slice of white bread.
What else is there to do
when her insides
have come unstitched
like an old cloth doll.
Now, she has toppled
from sitting position,
her cheek flush
against the seat cushion,
limbs too heavy to lift,
head sprouting white fuzz.

January Pearson / Orange, California

Edgar, Later (D. W. Griffith, 1909) / Nina Rao

In the gathering dark of her hair
her dress is the last thing visible, white
against a diminishing aperture.
Everything else has been a construction.
The lover or the envelope of money
always arrives after the heroine has died,
in poverty, not knowing. He knows.
He does not let anyone cut his hair.
Around them the future is descending like snow,
blanketing the cabin, although they don't speak of it,
or the way the starlings have gone silent outside.
In nature there are no doors except those
which creatures cut into the fabric of each other.
He thinks: *when she is dead* but then
all the verticals of the room go horizontal
so he has to stop and begin again: *when I
am dead* but this is like staring into the dark,
at night, sitting up in bed,
trying to make shapes out of the living dark.
In this he is continually distracted. Night,
starlings, white dress and future
descending like snow. There are things he sees
only in mirrors, or not at all

   Nina Rao / Atlanta, Georgia

Autumn, Fall / Robert Nisbet

Summer this year has ripened lustily,
the growth, the green, the tubers, the blooms.
We have known completeness.

Emlyn has been working on his cottage,
making it again a habitation and a home.
In the dust and cement, in the mixing air,
he has sawn and crafted, the planks,
the dovetails, the taps and the wiring.
In the fall Joan will be coming over,
the American girl.

When we sink into autumn, if you drive
the Aber road, passing below his cottage,
Emlyn's and Joan's place now,
you'll see, on the hill's flank,
the gleaming of their evening lights,
until they dip to darkness at eleven
and the hibernating night, the turning year,
will breed, brood.

   Robert Nisbet / Haverfordwest, Wales

Just Off the High Street / Robert Nisbet

In the Empire Cinema, a little Disney,
Jungle Cruise. Then, the prehistoric Croods.
Further along the High Street,
Superdrug and clothing places, Gregg's.
Briefly, the lovely local Sheep Shop,
before the Car-phone Warehouse, PC World,
and somehow the sense that lingering near us
is an age of haze, of spinning images,
our lives in a global wrap.

Rounding the corner, out of High Street,
almost a dog-leg, to a semi-alleyway
and small Victorian terraces. Here,
in this one window, right by the pavement,
perched on the sill, a globe,
slightly dusty and I can't quite see
just how much red is dotted round
its surface. In the room within
(but hey, come on, hell's bells,
you don't stare in at people's windows),
within … well, maybe this …
a ghostly schoolchild, pointing a compass,
dotting the globe, spinning it, intrigued,
peering a way around its empires,
its places and its fixity.

   Robert Nisbet / Haverfordwest, Wales

Branches and Windows / Christopher Woods

Photograph

Christopher Woods / Chappell Hill, Texas

In Margherita's Kingdom / Cate McGowan

After the photograph by Mario Lasalandra (1967)

Here, what cheer? The sorceress hears of hills that grow books.
Jigs and rhymes—saddle-shoe lost time. Bleached crinolines,
a photo's chockablock hole-shots, faint letters pop-locked, unshook.

Here, she spells sin, curses cliffs, bans noisome nooks,
spindrifts brine, that gray grind, the old tides' boss.
Hear, what cheer, the sorceress hears of hills that grow books.

There, a hedge-cloud. A noon shadow falls, hears no hook.
Ring bells, carillons on-the-brook. Toll, tarot sorceress,
a photo's chockablock, hole-shots feint, letters pop-locked. Unshook.

Here, she spiders cobwebs, quivers maps, witch silk unspooked.
Hear spooled jetties, tide pools, tadpoles that churn and toss
here. What cheer, the sorceress hears of hills that grow books.

Hear tall-tales she tells, spills such terms, such sorcery cooks.
Here, rhymes aperture, don f-stop chokers. Le juju albatross—
a photo's. Chockablock hole. Shots, feint. Letters pop, locked, un.
Shook.

Hear libraries spout gibberish, all manner of gobbledygook.
See. Have a look. There, there, tossed contrapposto, criss-crossed
here. What cheer the sorceress hears of hills that grow books,
a photo's chockablock hole-shots, faint letters pop-locked, unshook.

Cate McGowan / Maitland, Florida

That December / Peggy Hammond

began with no warning
of endings. Chilled mornings,
frost, white and shining,
crystallized grass crunching
like bones beneath our feet
as we ran for the bus,
mothers' thin voices trailing us.

Streaming through tiled hallways,
diverging like rivulets
into pools of classrooms,
we peeled away coats,
feeding them to open mouths
of cubbies crowned by names
on blue plastic strips.

Teachers herded us through lessons,
excitable colts, bucking, prancing,
our wild eyes flitting to salvation,
a red and green poster counting down
days to Christmas break.

Finally the last day.
Standing beside you, your voice
softening on my name, untamed
black hair, lopsided smile,
brown eyes kissed on one temple
by a tiny scar, a waning moon.

How much vacation had passed
when the call came? Your cousin,
his father's gun, shiny, tempting.
How he didn't know it was loaded.
How a bullet violated your slender throat.

At forty-three, I visit your faded gray stone;
my eyes trace lichen-filled lines
called for an angel, aged eleven,
linger on the etched lamb,
all the *nevers* of your life
woven in its tender wool.

    Peggy Hammond / Arden, North Carolina

L'Amour / Jane Blanchard

French lore maintains a hazel tree
likes extraordinarily

to have a honeysuckle vine
grow near enough to intertwine

so that the latter comes to love
the hold the former has dreamed of

and neither wants to live without
the other very close about.

    Jane Blanchard / Augusta, Georgia

Must Be the Wind / Jack Granath

You clean buildings at night. Solitary work with a mop bucket on wheels that creak. It's one o'clock, three o'clock in the morning, and a toilet flushes or the elevator rises. Of course, the building sits on an Indian burial ground. There is the story of the nun. The owner being frugal (and elsewhere), the lights are kept off except for every fifth fluorescent. One of them trembles as if shaken by footsteps upstairs. You would be frightened if it weren't for the thousands of other nights on the job. Still, you do avoid elevators because of the way the doors open, and anything could be there. In all those years how many sounds did you identify? A few broken fan belts and rattling pipes. Only once did you trace a crash to an intruder. You shouted, "Hey!" and the next day they called you a hero. Later that same year, a short circuit in the silent alarm brought three police officers with their guns drawn. Nobody called you a hero then. In one building the boss's son romanced his girlfriends in dark offices and made clinking sounds with bottles, but that was easier for you. That was known. Except for the one time, when you learned later that he hadn't been there, had been out of town all week. But the sounds are never the worst. Half-ghost yourself, you are not an occupant, so they set the HVAC to unoccupied. You wear gloves with no fingers in winter. You have seen your breath in basements. And then, shivering in that cold, you move through a warm spot in an empty hall, no explanation. In summer it's the opposite. You sweat and sometimes wipe your brow with a greasy rag and just then feel a coolness on the back of your neck like the mist from an eldritch waterfall. It doesn't last. You are seasoned. You have known a thousand scurryings, the indisputable clank of chain, the warm spot and the cool spot. Still, you do avoid elevators. And when you dig through the large canvas basket full of rags and come up against something solid that shouldn't be there, you do draw back and take a breath before investigating, before you ascertain: long-lost flashlight or human hand.

Jack Granath / Shawnee, Kansas

Painting Woman / Rana Williams

Photograph

Rana Williams / Hayesville, North Carolina

Time at the River / Mary McCarthy

Where dragonflies make quick stitches
in a crazy quilt pieced of sweet
evening blues, each shade
a reflection of memory;
some like pale silk, smooth
as a bride's wedding train,
some plush and thick as velvet,
others full of light, winking
like sequins on dark cloth, or sunlight
glinting off the rims
of a thousand small waves-

Here my thoughts move slow
as a hand stroking rich fabric,
acknowledging each stitch,
each odd shape made to fit my days,
and though this patchwork grows
to cover the river
and blanket the sky,
I know when I have had my fill of silence
it will fold up small enough
to carry back with me
into the noisiest narrow room.

   Mary McCarthy / Edgewater, Florida

Dandelion / Leslie Schultz

Taproot half-burrowing under pavement;
scorned by gardeners seeking flawless lawns,
showier blooms, more sweet, succulent fruit;

named "dog pisses" by Italian housewives
(messy yellow puddles near tidy streets);
still you offer every sharp excellence .

to the discerning eye and utile-aligned mind.
Your roasted root? A coffee substitute.
Your leaves? Delectable fried or steamed.

All of you, ground, makes a blood-tonic tea,
diuretic bitter herbal. Even
the leaky latex of your pink-green stems,

so bitter on an unsuspecting child's tongue,
has commercial value, might someday yield
accessible, perennial rubber.

Today, o maligned yet excellent plant,
I come to praise your keen-toothed survival,
your sheer, tough doggedness, your seasonal

transformation from compact golden suns
to silky-silvered parachuting moons.

    Leslie Schultz / Northfield, Minnesota

Leslie's poem is the winner of this issue's 50/50 poetry contest. She wins a check for half the entry fees and a one year subscription to the print edition of 3rd Wednesday.

Formal Imitation / Mark Mitchell

Only to hear
the call of a foghorn.
we cuffed you in bridges.

San Francisco sings
under a masked moon.

Only to hear
a foghorn's silver call,
your hills tense, shake, shrug.

San Francisco sighs
indifferent as a found cat.

Only to hear
a moon call from foghorns
we conjure the flesh songs
from all your haunted houses.

    Mark Mitchell / San Francisco, California

I Spent the Day in Armageddon / Emily Eddins

I spent the day in Armageddon
The blood-soaked sky
Maroon noon dark as night
The evening frogs, confused and chirping
We stumbled around
In our N95 masks
Gasping for fresh air
Submerged in smoke
I carefully strapped a filter
On my youngest child
Before he went outside to
Breathe the ash floating like
Flakes of snow and
Snap pictures to share
On social media
"Look at this strange day!"
The caption read
His childish enthusiasm
Smashed my heart
As if we were tourists to climate change
Instead of permanent residents
I guess it was sort of like
The Grand Canyon
You had to see it in person
To capture its immensity
Awe-inspiring angry earth
On fire and flashing red
A warning light to say good night
Glaring hot and obvious
To those in mourning.

   Emily Eddins / Atherton, California

To the Cats That Slink Out of Sight When I'm Walking in the Early Morning / Tom Large

Dear furry darlings, I don't mind
when you slip into the shadows
and Ignore my warmest greeting.
If you have been disturbed
in the middle of some amorous pursuit, I apologize.
To be caught when the lights come on
can be embarrassing.
Who wouldn't leap up and out of sight?
And if you were just about to eat
this fresh-killed furry thing
I'm stepping over on the sidewalk,
I'm sorry to interrupt your meal.
I hate settling down to dinner
Only to have the doorbell ring.

Of course there is no obligation
that you be warm and welcoming,
but if you've spent the night locked out,
irritably meowling round the neighborhood,
and no one let you in
I'm someone you could turn to now,
a leg to nudge your head against
a hand to gently rub your ears,
all given with great respect,
absolutely no strings attached.

   Tom Large / Baltimore, Maryland

Lord, Just Give Me One More Spring / Grey Held

Let me enter the backyard tool shed's faint dark,
take in rich rank smells of mulch,
whiffs of gas fumes from the tan
I'll tilt to fill the mower's throat.

Let me feel the demanding handles of hefty shovels,
the rough shank of my old rake,
the flat tires on my wintered-over bike,
the chains' stiff links craving oil.

Let me gorge myself on chores:
fix the spigot's drip, patch sidewalk cracks,
replace the split picket on the rickety fence,
tighten the loose lip of the brass latch,
scrub the musty beach-chair webbing
wedded by rivets to the frame,
fill holes dug by snakes and moles in the curved berm.

Let the crows come back,
hawking their *caw-caw-caw* on power lines.
Let tribes of tiny ants line up troops by the driveway.
Let maple pollen wallow all over the windshields.

I'll take it all—invasive vines twining
the trellis, grass grubs, rain-riven gutters plugged.

   Grey Held / Newtonville, Massachusetts

It Was the Cauliflower That Kept Me From Sleep / Babo Kamel

hovering like a strange off-white brain
escaped from the failed autopsy of a poem
in my sixth grade classroom filled
with budding bullies. And that poor boy
who stuttered through every presentation,
his face like a pomegranate left too long
in the sun reading out loud the first verse
of the Highwayman getting stuck at *riding*
never making it to *the old inn-door.*
The bigger boys at the back snickered
while we girls looked down wishing
that moment would flit above our heads,
to fly out the window. Like a shadowed thing
my grandmother once chased with a broom
shouting *fledermoyz*, a bat! My twin brothers
screaming on cue from their cribs.
One of whom called me tonight
from the one room apartment his life
has become. We speak each day and replay
the past in which he resides. Lithium
turning the days into a fifty year doze. He loves
music, though, and sits outside his building
singing Carole King songs to himself. And when
I ask him if he talks to any of the other residents
he laughs and tells me he can't waste his time
discussing the price of oranges or a sale on soap.
Instead he studies Torah on taped recordings
from 1988, rocks in his chair. Tells me
how much he loves reruns of Rosanne. Recites
all the dialogue, the way he used to midnights
at Rocky Horror Picture Shows, all glitter
and song, the urgency of sex, the entire theater
breathing as one beautiful beast, unbusted.

When I Stop Being Her Daughter / Babo Kamel

The morning after Shiva
it's the requisite walk around the block.

Stratus clouds tease the winter sky
with a floating scarf of sorrow.

A minyan of sparrows descend
on a tree bereft of leaves.

Everything is the same and nothing
is the way it was before.

Crows cackle at some cruel joke.
I am its punchline.

A plastic bag branch-snagged
transforms into a strange beige lung.

My mother lies deep in the dark she was afraid of.
In the land of the dead there is only one season.

    Babo Kamel / Venice, Florida

City Snow / Margaret Birth

From my front window, I watch
sidewalk and street just outside succumb
to a shushing whisper of white,
and a line of cars slide to a deft stop—
despite slick-growing asphalt—
at the traffic light at the end
of my Queens, New York, block.

As the snow deepens, I hear
the whirring scream of wheels
trying to turn, but stuck in slippery ruts,
and an ash-gray sky seems
to lower and wrap itself around
cheek-by-jowl houses
and winter-leafless trees.

That evening, we walk to Mass; I feel
my feet sink into drifts beyond ankle-deep.
Evening Mass is minus the music
of the organ; of whooshing breezes,
however, we have a chorus.
Christmas candlelight from the Advent
wreath flickers shadows over the few worshipers.

Exiting an hour later, we see
that nighttime darkness has overtaken dusk: streetlights illuminate
flying, stinging flakes, even as cars have deserted the roadways.
Our family pushes through piles of frigid
whiteness—sidewalks where snow has drifted—then
decides to take advantage of rare city peace
and make a path home down the middle of newly plowed streets.

   Margaret Birth / South Ozone Park, New York

Sweeping Under the Rug / Gary Bloom

Photograph

Gary Bloom / Pass Christian, Mississippi

Facsimile / Ruth Bavetta

I was here before everything
changed. Before the redbird

turned to black, before the lilies
lied, and the tides turned hot.

Before you receded into photographs.
Before bread turned to sawdust,

eggs to tears. The patina of loss
is stitched in rags.

    Ruth Bavetta / San Clemente, California

Light Likes / Ryan Brennan

Light likes the hair of the willow
the blue green needles of pine
creases in the river current
our kitchen in the morning
silvery undersides of vultures
wicks of dew after a summers rain
factory windows at sunset
and the tenuous threads of spiders
barely seen in the wind

    Ryan Brennan, Woodstock, New York

Plumbing / Sally Zakariya

The plumber comes to deal with the shower

We see him once or twice a year
this slight, dark man from Ethiopia

When he's done he joins us for a cup of tea
strokes the cat, murmurs in its ear

I want to ask him about the civil war
raging in his country but instead
I say how I admire the churches
cut from living bedrock

They're built by angels, the story goes

I picture cherubim with hammers and chisels
carving out a haven for the spirit

I've never been to Lalibela, he says
I hope someday to go there

Meanwhile he scours down clogged drains
to clear away the detritus of life

    Sally Zakariya / Arlington, Virginia

Walk, Swim, Fly / Sally Zakariya

The sun slants in on the *Times,* which informs me
I share some cellular history with insects and fish –
DNA that tells us whether to grow legs
or fins or wings

I try to imagine the ancestors who handed down
those what-will-it-be genes

Why not wings for me, I wonder, why not
legs for the cuttlefish, fins for the fly

Mother Nature is a jokester, but I knew
that already, having spent years coddling
hips and knees that don't want to last
as long as the rest of me

Maybe bipedalism isn't all it's cracked up to be

Maybe evolution had other ideas for us

Or maybe we humans are just living past
our sell-by date

    Sally Zakariya / Arlington, Virginia

Salad Nicoise, 2019 / Sinclair Buckstaff
(Honorable Mention in 3W's Annul Fiction Contest)

Hal was eating a Salad Nicoise, not because he wanted to, but because his wife, Doris, had ordered it for him. Hell, he didn't even know what a Salad Nicoise was. But he was eating it. And he was eating it left-handed. He looked at his right hand resting in his lap tranquilly, uselessly. When he was young, playing football, he was what they called "country strong." During haying season on the ranch he had walked along next to the truck and heaved bales up onto its platform all day long. He'd do it with his left hand leading for a while and then switch to his right hand leading for a while so that he developed strength equally on each side of his body. It built up his legs, his arms, and his torso. Opposing linemen were child's play by comparison. Now his right arm just hung there and his right leg lagged.

There had been multiple months of painful rehabilitation and therapy sessions and many, too many, appointments with Hal's doctor, an old friend from high school who had gone away to college and medical school, interned in the big city on the opposite side of the state, and then returned to the little town of his youth to bring his medical knowledge to the community that still had the greatest hold on his heart. He and Hal had been bookend anchors on the line for their conference-winning football team their senior year. At the most recent appointment Doris had asked the question most concerning to her and Hal.

"Will he improve?"

"Nope." Turning and looking directly at Hal, Doc said softly, "I'm sorry, but this is the new normal, 'ol Buddy."

Well at least he doesn't equivocate, thought Hal. Where did *that* word come from? He'd always thought it was a way of bragging to use a fifty-cent word when a five-cent word would do just as well. Now his mind was trying to slip those fifty-cent words in.

Doc said a diet too rich in the things he liked to eat had caused it. That and a family predisposition and a bunch of other factors Hal didn't care to dwell on. None of that mattered now.

Doris had chosen the restaurant precisely because it wasn't one of his favorites. It was new, the talk of the county on account of the trendy food it prepared. What mattered to Doris was that it served dishes *other* than those that had taken Hal down. When they ordered the main course Doris did the talking. She asked his opinion, of course, but when she made a suggestion, he just nodded.

Hal looked at Doris. She was trying so hard. It had to be difficult, wearing, to try to keep up both ends of every conversation between them these days. God knows she was a feisty little thing. They'd always scrapped, and she had always given as good as she got. That was part of the attraction. And that was one of the things that bothered him so much about this thing. He couldn't give as good as *he* got anymore. And then there was the note of solicitousness that had crept into her voice. Solicitousness? Now there was a word for you. How had that come up out of his addled brain? In any case, he hated it.

When the main course was finished, the waiter asked, "Would you like dessert?"

Hal's eyes lit up, and Doris saw it.

"Do you have cheesecake?"

"Yes."

"Good. Then we'll split a piece of cheesecake."

Split? Hal tried not to show his disappointment.

"Does that come with fresh fruit on it?" Doris quickly asked.

"We can prepare it that way. Would strawberries work?"

Strawberries—his favorite.

"Yes, that would be perfect."

While they waited for dessert to arrive old acquaintances stopped by their table on the way out.

"Good to see you out and about, Hal. Haven't seen you in a while. On the mend?"

"Oh, yes," Doris answered affirmatively. Hal didn't respond. He saw their eyes, knew what they were thinking, and didn't like it.

"That was nice of them to stop by," Doris said after they had left. Hal didn't respond.

At least there was a full reservoir upstream of the hay fields—the life insurance was current, the note against the ranch was paid off, and the kids were grown and could fend for themselves. Dan, the oldest, pretty well ran the operation these days. William—Bill—was a lawyer of all things, and a successful one at that. And Molly, like a lot of women, had married her father, or a reasonable facsimile of him. Her husband was big, a rancher, and they fought like cats and dogs, too. He smiled a crooked smile at the thought.

"What?" Doris asked. He gave a small shake of his head, as if to say, "Oh, nothing."

Outside, after the meal, they walked slowly toward where the car was parked. It wasn't far. Doris had been careful about that. They only had one intersection to cross. A fully-loaded logging truck was coming and pretty fast. It was trying to beat the red light on the traffic signal cycle. It'd do the trick. Hal waited until it got close, and then he stepped out in front of it.

    Sinclair Buckstaff / Jackson, Wyoming

The Seventh Age / Hattie Clarke

Curled like an ampersand
over a bowl of soup
she snips bits of air from the space before her
and places them on her tongue.
Her grandchildren think her mad
not knowing that August tastes of lemon
and January of rock candy.
She sleeps with her face nestled against a gray cat
another folded across her chest
thrumming his happiness
reminding her heart of its obligation.

Her children think her sorrowful.
They don't know
that she sifts through the buttons in the jar
because she finds them beautiful.
She's lost something, they say.
When in fact she's found the secret.

    Hattie Clarke / Marietta, Ohio

Autumn, Departures / Robert Haight

In October you might
not notice the silence
right away in the morning
when light has illuminated
the trees and grass
before sunrise.
You might not notice
the months long song of crickets
has ended, blown off
with the cool breeze,
that the garble of song birds
in the spruces and pines
has flown south.
The leaves stir,
some whisking away
down the street
as if they too had a date
with migration.
The gulls have left wrappers
they picked clean on the beach.
It might be then you notice
that man from down the dirt road
who walked his dog a few mornings
a week has been gone for months,
that his name on the pole barn
was removed last spring,
and you might remember
that lovely woman
who worked at the dry cleaner,
always wearing a dress and jewelry
as if she were headed to a party
some weekday morning,
is no longer there.
The crows remain through the cold.
They watch you with a wary eye.
They remember your face.

An Empty Field / Robert Haight

The grass has grown long
where Red's house used to be,
some deer trails running through it
to the overgrown shrubs
he used to trim, the flowers
he tended smothered by wild
flowers, chicory, carrot, yarrow
the colors of late summer sky
and clouds.

The driveway is still there
under it all, broken pieces
of cement leading nowhere
with the meadow all around.
After Red drove the wrong way
down I-94 to get his license
renewed, went missing for a few
days and got found by the cops,
they took him away.
His dog too, we hope.

A few months later
the empty house burned down,
early morning, no one around.
Now it's just a field in the grasslands
full of crickets and grasshoppers
chirping and ticking all day long.

    Robert Haight / Marcellus, Michigan

Angel of Death / Mary Stebbins Taitt

Scratchboard and Mixed Media

Mary Stebbins Taitt / Grosse Pointe Farms, Michigan

Old Man Taking Account / Darrell Petska

(a *greguería*)

Foot, clawed, just out of reach, known for going where no man
had any business going, has an identical twin just as flat and slow.

Ankles, accessories to feet and just as guilty, twisted, sprained, screwed,
inflexible, arthritis the wages of past imprudence.

Knees, rickety as autumn's reed, bitter complainers at the slightest
elevation change, quick to surrender, braced, inflamed, scalpel-bound.

Hip, hip hooray, one repaired, one to go still catching and popping,
ancient hippie hinge forbidden the lotus pose and Kama Sutra sex.

Back, fickle, treasonous, unbending even to a grandkid's "up,"
a chiropractor's dream, pass the Percocet, no longer doing honey-do.

Eyes, can't see you, where's the magnifying glass, speak up,
ears can't hear you, sitting alone in a room filled with others.

Mind, a futile trap, losing words and memories like rats fleeing a sunk
ship, photo album fanatic, sudokued, crossword-crazed, duly sticky-noted.

Hands, the torturer's handiwork, gnarled, helpless before jar lids, reaching
to touch and be touched, still raising the middle finger death's way.

Heart, firing on three pistons, achy-breaky, long repair record, spark-
plugged, fueled with love and grandkids, running the beater into the ground.

Darrell Petska, Middleton, Wisconsin

Editor's Note: This may be our first ever *greguería*.

Everything Depends on the Day You Ask Me / Ronda Broatch

How the forest calls, golden hour mixing with dew
seeping through hemlock and cedar, the tall firs,
searching the fern-strewn floor like a ghost appearing

only in light. I'd get my camera, but remain
rooted, knowing an instant makes a difference,
that witness endures beyond pixel and print.

When the retrospective of What I Missed opens
at the End-of-Life Museum, the fermentation of experience,
my finest moments distilled to a shadow-

box of black birds, my mother's fears, my father's
spent inheritance. Everything depends on
how you sing, how you ask a raincloud for more

time. Nothing hangs on a paper clip, but it is stapled
to the heart's to-do list, and maybe the blackbird isn't really
screaming, but trying to warn us that happiness lies

in the stars of dogwood, beneath fern where the junco dwells,
that songs live in a back pocket and the envelopes
of sleep, washed to fading over the years. Loam

older than we are. Water dripping from the Douglas firs.
I hold a mirror to the sky, that I might see you more clearly.

   Ronda Broatch / Kingston, Washington

Growing Gone / Kevin Brown

It was Thursday.

Kalem was supposed to fly down to El Paso the next morning to see his father and baby half-sister. It had been eight years since he'd last seen or spoken to the old man. The year Kalem had grown stubble on his chin. His dad had gone out for a few minutes and stayed out forever.

But last week, the phone rang and it was him. Calling to say he'd gotten remarried three years ago. A Mexican girl he'd met on vacation in Chihuahua. Said they were living in El Paso and just had a daughter.

"You're a big brother," he said. His voice sounded as it had years ago—liquored.

So Kalem was going to fly down and do eight years' worth of playing father and son. They planned to drive up to Tombstone, Arizona. Check out the O.K. Corral. His dad had become an Old West aficionado.

"Wyatt Earp. Billy the Kid. The outlaws," he said. "That all happened out here."

After they hung up, Kalem booked a flight, his hands trembling the phone against his ear.

Now it was Thursday, and he'd been calling his dad for two days to tell him it was all set. He couldn't get an answer. Earlier that morning, the answering machine apologized but informed him that the inbox was full.

He called his grandmother to see if she knew what was going on.

"Oh, honey, it's awful," she said. "Just awful. He's done it now."

"Done what?" Kalem said.

"Messed around and got caught with dope."

"He what?" Kalem said, no breath in his voice. "What kind of dope?"

"That cocaine. Down there in Mexico, trying to bring back a bagful. Got pulled over stateside. Had it in his muffler." She sighed and Kalem could tell she'd been crying. He'd never heard her cry, even times when she should have. "Says he didn't know it was in there, but sure enough…"

"What about the baby?" Kalem said, almost saying "my sister."

"Her mom took and ran off with her. Cops are trying to find them." She sniffled and her voice broke. "He's looking at three to five years in jail."

And that was that. Trip off. Reunion incarcerated.

Kalem hung up and looked at himself in the mirror. At the trimmed hair on his face. Eight years of beard had come and gone and come again. He wondered about the little girl, his baby sister, living a childhood of hiding. Of being an outlaw and not having a father. He wondered if she could do it. He hoped she would.

He picked up the phone to cancel his flight. He knew *he* could do it. It was just time and you adjust to anything with time. Waiting for the airline agent to pick up, he scratched his beard and smiled. He could do three to five years with his hands cuffed behind his back.

   Kevin Brown / Bella Vista, Arizona

Deer in the Yard / J. R. Solonche

I once heard someone say
That they're nothing but
giant rats with hooves. He
has a point. They're pests all
right. They eat everything,
including what the gardening
books say they don't. And
there's no denying that they're
hazards on the roads. I see them
everywhere, especially now in
the middle of autumn, their dead
bodies contorted every which way.
But look at this one. Look at how
she looks at me. Look at how she
stands there. Look at how she
holds her ground. Look at how
the right foreleg starts to move,
then stops moving. Look at how
she wants to take one step forward,
one step toward me, but doesn't.
This is my ground, she says.
Look at how I hold it.

    J.R. Solonche / Blooming Grove, New York

I Do Not Wish Them Ill / J. R. Solonche

I do not wish them ill,
but I have a confession to make.
I hope Sosler's Farm Equipment
on Route 17M between Goshen
and Middletown never sells
these gleaming, brand new, bright
red tractors lined up in a perfect
row like toy soldiers on parade,
tin British grenadiers in their
immaculate crimson in front
of Buckingham Palace. Let them
sell all the others, the green
and yellow John Deeres, the white
and orange International Harvesters,
the Massey Fergusons, the Cases.
I don't care. It's the red ones I will
miss when they are gone, sold off
one by one. It's the red ones I will
miss the way I already miss the heart-
stopping redder than red tulips in my
garden the deer ate, one by one, last year.

J. R. Solonche / Blooming Grove, New York

Interiors / David Chorlton

It's dark in here; can't see the sky
Tom Russell, Blue Wing

The shower's filled with plastic bags, a box
for storing files, a colander, cloths and rags and
all to overflowing where
there's no room left for water, just
the shape of a cutout pine tree hanging
from a rail to freshen the air.
Piled upon the kitchen stove are plastic sacks,
a dustpan, boxes filled with mystery, rags
and secrets that close with a snap
when the lid is pressed down. Manila
folders stacked in a side room collect
the dust that hasn't settled on
magazines and cartons and an obsolete
laptop in a pile too challenging to
explore, with a black-and-red carrier
for one of the cats that came
every day to the backyard for food,
floating on a paper tide. A desperate chandelier
struggles to illuminate the waves
of books and bags and bottles and boxes
upon which a red plastic dish for feeding
sails bravely on towels and old clothes
toward the island with its stacks
of case files and the inaccessible far wall
upon which hang the framed views
of the world outside, where even
the Safeway pigeons make a bright wave that dips
and rises as they sweep back to the roof
when a Cooper's Hawk comes down
riding on a raindrop's back.

David Chorlton / Phoenix, Arizona

Monarch / David Chorlton

Infinity's a play of light and shade today, clouds
strung peak to peak along
the mountain ridge, and the moon
a scimitar at dawn
when yesterday's melancholy
dissolves to let the sunrise through.
The flowering bushes fill with Arizona
Sister, Viceroy and Red Admiral: heartbeats
in flight and banners from the spirit world
when they stop
to hang from a leaf. What was done was
done and dusted long ago, before
this morning's Monarch
landed on a flower and spoke in black
and orange of the journey
through time with no end in sight, only
the trembling in
its *follow me* wings.

    David Chorlton / Phoenix, Arizona

Away We Go / Robert Bulman

on this glorious day
in this Oregon July
with forests alive
and the river free
an empty raft
floats downstream
peacefully
on the Deschutes

eight ex-passengers
lava chewing at their shins
desperately try to remember
how to survive-
float on your back
feet forward
don't panic

settling into the raft,
in the pre-trauma dawn
an anxious boy, still innocent
strapped on bravery
like a life jacket
and asked a childish question
what happens if
the boat tips over?

once in a thousand trips, they say
just one in a thousand
pretty good odds
so don't you worry
just wedge in your feet
tighten your vest
and away we go

in a raft
not yet empty

    Robert Bulman / Davis, California

Micro-sociology / R. A. Allen

While wasting an afternoon at the sidewalk café
I watched him watch his waitress saunter away.
He was that cartoon wolf in a zoot suit.
He was front-page tabloid sex-guilt.
Hc was The Lecher of Wakefield.
Noticing me, his wife noticed him.
(He studied his menu like a Trappist novitiate.)
She nailed me for complicity,
and, in the heat of her insecticidal stare,
I squirmed like a thing Kafkaesque.

    R. A. Allen / Memphis, Tennessee

Landing in Is / Lily Jarman-Reisch

> after "The Land of Is" by Stephen Dunn

His accent tells me he is Greek,
asks if he may have the seat next to mine.
Vevea, I say. Of course.
Milate Ellinika? he asks. Do you speak Greek?
A tilt of my head tells him I do.

We speak Greek all the way to New York,
he a scholar of classics,
ancestral dances of Chios.
We will go there together,
he whispers, after our second glass of wine.
He talks of lemon groves under Kimomeni,
her slopes stippled titian with poppies,
says we will wake to bells on donkeys laden
with loaves of Paschal bread,
roast a lamb fragrant with wild thyme
to light turning pink-gold to indigo,
climb to the monastery at midnight
through forests flickering with honey-hued fruit,
scent of citrus freed by a yellow sun.

The plane touches down at La Guardia,
glides to the gate,
passengers pad off the plane.
An old Hassid in the next seat elbows me,
eager for home.
On my tongue a rind of lemon
from my long-empty water glass.

> Lily Jarman-Reisch / Baltimore, Maryland

Christmas Crow / Lynn White

We watched the crow with fascination
as it tap tapped on the window pane,
saw its black eyes gleaming,
its wet feathers shining
in the moonlight.
And we understood.

We understood that it wanted to join us,
to perch among the baubles
on our shining tree
to share our fireside warmth
on Christmas Eve
and escape
the cold winter rain.

We heard it promise
to sing for us
We opened the window
and let it in.
It crowed a Christmas carol.

Lynn White / Blaenau Ffestiniog, United Kingdom

Think (Always) / Patricia Bingham

Drawing

Patricia Bingham / Pocatello, Idaho

Moth Wings / Laura Ann Reed

When are we going home, he asks
like a child who's had enough
of the windy beach,
the playground swings
and slide.
He's dying of pneumonia
and a failing heart.
Propped up in bed
between pale green walls
he glides in and out of delirium.
I take his hand, the skin cool and dry,
tissue-thin.
At the window a tiny moth
batters himself
like a dusty saint
against the pane.
From across the room my father calls,
Sweetheart, when?
as if the way out or in
is glassy and brief—
a wingbeat.

    Laura Ann Reed / Mill Creek, Washington

Splintered White Picket Fence / Victoria Melekian

I come from a long line of women
who check for a murderer lurking

behind the shower curtain,
who worry about tetanus and polio,

bees swarming the front porch,
women who passed down their angst,

their strength and independence,
women who taught me well:

if your heart's stuck in a cheese grater,
hide it in the kitchen drawer. Fold your anger

into a napkin and get the kids to school.
Smile through prickly silences and never

ladle family secrets into a stranger's bowl.
Take a small gift when visiting and pay

your own way. Go beyond ordinary
and extend your Sunday best.

Run with scissors if necessary,

write it across the steamy mirror
in the morning and believe it all day.

    Victoria Melekian / Carlsbad, California

Love Blind / Shannon Hollinger

A grey cloud of exhaust eddies across the lane as the rusty pick-up settles to a halt. Battle worn hinges creak as the door opens, groans with relief as it shuts. John Willis trudges down the path towards the dock, kicking pebbles and stirring dust clouds with each step as he walks under the wizened oaks that line the trail. Their solemn sentry reminds him of inmates, wordlessly watching from their cells as a fellow felon made the final walk to the death chamber.

John's work boots thud hollowly across the planks of the dock, the weathered wood bleached like bone. Reaching the end, he sits down beside Lori and leans against a piling. He can feel the silence pressing against his skin like he's a lemon being juiced. Her scorn feels just as sour.

"Listen, Lori." Eyes squeezed shut, he pictures her face, every curve and line pressed deeply into the folds of his brain. "I'm sorry."

He swats absently at a mosquito buzzing near his ear. "I know I messed up. I handled everything all wrong. If I could go back and change things, I would."

The drone of the insect grows louder. He swings at the bug before slapping the dock beside his leg. The wood splinters under his palm, probing his flesh with sharp teeth. It makes his skin itch. "I know I shouldn't have done what I did, but damn it, Lori, I was afraid of losing you. What was I supposed to do?"

The water laps against the dock pilings, caressing them gently. The light reflecting from the surface of the lake plays across John's face, flashing like fish scales. "What's done's been done."

Sighing deeply, he raises his face to the sun, squinting against the brightness. "It's gonna be a nice day. Not too much of summer left. You should try and enjoy it."

The wind whispers through the leaves. John rubs his hands nervously over his thighs and leans forward. His eyes follow the piling beside him down to where it disappears into the murky water. Right at the line where the light and the dark collide, he can just see a few tendrils of hair floating up toward him, waving like fingertips. "Well, I've got to get to work. I'll be back to see you tomorrow. You take care, now."

With a groan John rises to his feet and slowly retreats to his truck. He can't see the wrath in those wisps of hair as the water current whips them into a frenzy. But he can feel it. He yanks the truck door open and climbs inside. A rip in the vinyl seat presses hard into the back of his thigh, but he doesn't notice. His fingers wrap around the steering wheel, his lips curling into a grin. "I knew it," he says softly, smiling as his head shakes slowly from side to side. "You do still love me. You couldn't be this damn mad at me if you didn't."

   Shannon Hollinger / Indialantic, Florida

Do the Storms Still Reach You? / John Tustin

Does the water still run
all along
the four sides of your bed
when you sleep at night
with eyes shut too tight,
lovely eyebrows arched
like guardrails against
the encroaching sunlight?

Do your bedsheets wrinkle now?
Do you still listen to the music
of the bedraggled
and think of me?
Do you hide your memories of me
under the floorboards
beside your talismans
and your sex dreams?

Has the ocean gotten
farther away
or is it you
who's moved inland?
Do the storms still reach you?
Does your man help you
close all the windows
and apply your earplugs
when the thunder roars,
sounding like the noises
we once made together?

It's raining here now
and its smell
reminds me of your
spirals of hair
 your spiral staircase
the spirals of smoke
you used to call me
to come to you
when you wanted me –
back when I'd lie beside you,
watching your eyebrows knit
in the dark:
back
before I acquired
all these questions.

John Tustin / Myrtle Beach, South Carolina

Words / Gary Wadley

Drawing

le retired Dutch valleys, found here and there embosomed
te of New York, that population, manners, and cust
d; while the great torrent of migration and improveme
king such incessant changes in other parts of this rest
eeps by them unobserved. The are like those little nooks
ich border a rapid stream; w e may see the straw and
 quietly at anchor, or in their mimic ha
bed by the rush of t. Though many
psed since I trod th des o Sleepy Hollow, ye
ether I should still trees the same f
ing in its
In this by-place remote period
tory, that is to say, ce, a rthy wight
Ichabod ressed it,
epy Hollo children of
 was a nati supplies the
ineers for the st, and sends
legions of fro l-masters. T
Crane was n was tall, bu
k, with narr gs, hands th
le out of his served for sho
ole frame m ad was smal
, with huge long snipe
ooked like ndle neck,
y the wind see him striding he profile c
idy day, with his clothes bagging and fluttering about hir
ve mistaken him for the genius of famine descending up
some scarecrow eloped from a corn-field.
His school-house was a low building of one large room

Gary Wadley / Louisville, Kentucky

Dad and the Gates of Hell / Ruth Holzer

The movers in their emptied van
are on the road back to N..J.
where Dad himself will not return,
except for the last time
in his white pine box.
But that is still a year or so away.

Now he's standing on the porch
among the geraniums and rocking chairs
as twilight deepens.
He says that when he moves again
he will be stripped of everything.
But that is for another day.

Now it's time for early dinner
with a crowd of shadowy residents
who come and go at such a pace
it would be senseless to make friends.
He steps across the threshold, muttering:
Abandon hope, all you who enter here.

Ruth Holzer / Herndon, Virginia

The Greyhound / **Graham C.** Goff

Clint delivered babies, stopped fights, and drove buses. Driving buses was what he was paid to do, but delivering babies and stopping fights was what he was expected to do. Clint did not mind his job as a Greyhound bus driver, but sometimes circumstances arose that required skills or patience above his pay grade. In these situations, took a smoke break or pretended to know what to do. Sometimes both. Clint did not mind his job as a Greyhound bus driver.

All the towns on Clint's route looked the same. Each had a dilapidated courthouse that had not been renovated in decades due to city budget shortfalls and a generalized sense of apathy towards the condition of local government buildings. Each had a church off the square that left its lights on through the night and a billboard with service times and a religious aphorism written in replaceable letters. Clint did not know who they were trying to advertise to. Had anyone ever attended a Sunday morning service on the basis of a witty church sign saying? Each town had a 24/7 diner by the bus station. They all had the same menu with slight variations in price and quality. Allensville had the best food but Brookdale had the best prices. They all had subpar customer service. All the people looked the same in each and none of them had attended a Sunday morning service on the basis of a witty church sign saying.

The people in the diners were indistinguishable from the people who Clint transported. This was partially because the diners got the majority of their early morning business from Greyhound riders, and partially because most people looked the same to Clint. Every bus had a drunk and a person experiencing some kind of withdrawals. Sometimes they were the same person and sometimes they sat together. Every bus had a woman with a child that she held close to her side like they might disappear at any moment. Every bus had someone reading the bible. Some were traveling missionaries. Some were looking for something to read. Maybe some had been convinced by a witty church sign, but Clint doubted it.

He needed coffee. It was late, or early, depending on one's reading of the time. Clint checked his watch as passengers began to file in. It was nearly departure time. He waited an extra minute and waved the stragglers in. They smelled like coffee and cigarettes and eggs and ketchup on hash browns and steak sauce on sausage. When everyone was seated, Clint backed out and continued down the highway, instinctively driving to Allensville. By the light of flickering street lamps, he discerned a city hall with a boarded window and a church with a sign that said something about Jesus and love. It wasn't very clever, but Clint was not going to visit anyway.

A man sat on an overpass over the highway, his legs dangling from the edge. His mouth moved like he was talking. He rocked back and forth on the ledge, but when he saw the Greyhound, he waved. Clint waved back and wondered why the man on the overpass was off his schedule; he was not supposed to be suicidal until the first Wednesday of the month. Maybe he could not pay his rent or had been dumped or wanted someone to talk him down. Clint watched the silhouette on the overpass until he was no longer visible. Maybe he just wanted someone to wave at.

   Graham C. Goff / Brownwood, Texas

Night Blizzard / Richard Schiffman

Shooting under street lamps,
a billion sideways-streaking comets,
shards of sky-lint, pods and packets of angel-dust,
little stars swelling as I sleep, sweeping all night,
silting gutters, smothering windshields, heaped
in snaking dunes, inch by inch, swaddling streets
and stalling buses. Inch by inch as I sleep,
as I huddle under covers, waking now and then
to watch it, though it does just fine without me.
Still I cannot help but part the blinds to peer
between the slats, to see if it's still falling.
A blizzard that does not need me to see it.
But it falls. It falls anyway. And it will still
be there at daybreak. Or the bone-white
aftermath. The glinting remnants
in the too-bright light of day.

    Richard Schiffman / New York, New York

First Love / Richard Schiffman

We called these London planes
"itchy ball trees" and pelted one another
with their barbed, testicular fruit.
Or we stripped off the jigsaw-puzzle bark
to carve our names in the moist cambium.
The big-hipped mamas survived
our adolescent crimes, even thrived
in the little sidewalk plots they were allotted.
They were our shade in summer,
in fall, a crown of crayon-yellow
quick to brown, in early spring,
the leaves were gold-green chrysalis.
But in winter, stripped and glistening,
the hulking trees moved a boy to pity.
When my buddies weren't looking,
I stroked the trunk, I stooped and kissed
some secret place of cleavage.
After a windstorm flipped one by the roots,
I lay there on the ground beside her, sap rising.

    Richard Schiffman / New York, New York

Boot Jack / Donald Wheelock

The oldest thing I own,
two rough-hewn scraps of wood:
one cut to grip the boot
snug to the ankle bone,

then nailed to an angled block
with hand-forged nails (and three
banged in more recently
from cut-nail hardware stock).

Some country craftsman's eye
saw in the needed use
a whimsical excuse
to hone and dignify:

for such a crude device
it has a fine detail,
makes of a swallow's tail
a grip of strength and grace.

But for its grace, I doubt
this jack would now exist,
endure a move, resist
the urge to throw it out.

Three hundred years and more
it's come through to fulfill
a task it's up to still,
stationed by the door.

    Donald Wheelock / South Deerfield, Massachusetts

Being Born / Jeremiah Durick

It's something we all experience but find
it hard to recall – that coming into all this
headfirst, our first feelings of separateness
even the loneliness we live with. All of our
senses working, the brightness, the wet feel
of it, even those odd senses, taste and smell,
but we have nothing to compare them to.
We hear our first sounds, people talking about
us, to us, but with words that remain strange
sounds. We blink, we move, and then most of
us begin to cry, our sounds sound right, say
how we feel about this. They weigh us, measure
us, clean us up, wrap us in womb-like warmth,
even give us our first hat to wear. We wear what
they give us, begin to think, notice things around
us, the people, then the important people. We
begin learning how to live the mystery of all this
and begin to become who we are. There's just
way too much to remember – so we don't.

   Jeremiah Durick / South Burlington, Vermont

Clue of Home / J. S. Absher
May 4, 2020

> *You think it is the bird which is free. Wrong: it is the flower.*
> —Reb Zale

For the first time in weeks I walk out
towards our ponds, now dull as muddy boots,
but in high summer the slime algae
will conjure a bright green. The mulberries
are pale, the mock strawberries blood red.

On the banks are yellow irises, oxalis
leaves as purple as old bruises, blooms
the white of clean bandages. Catchweed
ramps beside me, reaching out to grab
my pants-leg and go places.

But I don't go far or often. I read and watch.
In a show I'm binging, an L. A. detective
looks for a spent slug by raking detritus
aside with his foot. When he walks behind
the warty bark of a tree, I wonder, *Our*

hackberry or a lookalike? Memory goes
to places I've been, the once ordinary
rhythms of life, a family I visited
when I was 10—their almost cool, dew-
wet mornings and muggy afternoons,

the June bug's leg they tethered to a thread
while it tried to fly home, the buzz
of its little engine over revving.
I too was homesick, in agony,
especially the clammy nights.

In the harbor, near mothballed Liberties,
the father snagged a jellyfish with a stick,
pulled it out of the water, a snotty
handkerchief. I wanted to go home,
if home is the place you never have to leave.

   J. S Absher / Raleigh, North Carolina

I Knew Bobolinko in High School / Kenneth Pobo

At our 20th school reunion,
he seemed pretty much the same.
He stood by a punch bowl

clutching a *Butterfingers*. I told him
I had become a successful analyst.
He asked what did I analyze--

it was complicated. I offered him punch.
He said he hadn't become successful,
success being a train which can

hit you if you walk on the tracks.
Our mutual friend Sabine broke
into our chat. She said she was

quite successful—at being odd.
She hadn't changed. Bobolinko
looked like the picture of

a younger Eisenhower hanging
by the bathroom door.
He shrugged and left early.

Kenneth Pobo / Media Pennsylvania

Women These Days / Sarah Iler

He describes to me how
He has lost faith in women.
He tells me of the women who hurt him

In ways strikingly reminiscent
To the way he hurt me. It is silly and absurd,
Hard to believe he doesn't see.

But he does not. And in the meantime
He reminds the world again
And again, he isn't the one who should feel

Ashamed. He is enraptured in his own pain.
Entirely wrapped up in himself.
This is one of the things he hates

About women these days:
They are so self-centered, he says
Without a hint of irony in his voice.

    Sarah Iler / Blacksburg, Virginia

The Snake Man's Lesson / Robert Fillman

My neighbor Sid collected snakes,
had a basement filled with them, each
held in a house of glass. Sid walked
/
us down to watch him feed baby
mice to his saddle-brown boa.
He'd dangle a white creature by

its tail above the tank so we
could see its tiny pink eyes and
tiny pink ears twitching as it

struggled and thrashed to stay alive.
Sid's grip was firm in hand and mind.
His smile made us squirm, shield faces.

He would promise it was over,
get us to uncover our eyes
in time to see that muscular

shiny body coiling around
its motionless prey. Years later,
I learned he was a professor

of wildlife management. I guess
he wanted to teach us that death
meant life, show us every story
had two sides if we dared to look.

    Robert Fillman / Macungie, Pennsylvania

Team Captain / Virginia Smith

Your call to tell me
your sentencing was

quick, like most of your
rare reaches outward

to those who've stayed through
addiction, madness,

estrangement with you.
I hear you light a

cigarette as you
say 22 to

36 months, and
I wonder what those

offenders without
fancy lawyers, trust

funds, indulgent dads
do. Ten years, often.

I can't figure if
relief or self-pity or something

like sorrow
fills the phone. We light

on the difference
between surviving

and thriving in state
prison, what it might be.

You always flee and
hide, an animal

from a trap, a child
under the bed, though

now you're found and caught.
For comfort, I recall

you gliding the ice
faster, more graceful

than any, racing
from the penalty box

to hustle the puck,
break away, slide the

biscuit behind the
goalie, your face through

the bars of your helmet
happy, with nothing to lose.

Virginia Smith / Philadelphia, Pennsylvania

Drawing 2 / John Loree

John Loree (deceased) / Ypsilanti, Michigan

Made in the USA
Columbia, SC
01 December 2021